ROBERT QUACKENBUSH

THERE'LL BE A HOT TIME IN THE OLD TOWN TONIGHT

J.B. LIPPINCOTT COMPANY/PHILADELPHIA & NEW YORK

For our son Piet Robert
and for
firemen's children everywhere

U.S. Library of Congress Cataloging in Publication Data. Quackenbush, Robert M   There'll be a hot time in the old town tonight. SUMMARY: Illustrations accompany the verses of the folksong describing the Chicago fire. Includes the music and information on fire safety. [1. Folksongs, American] I. Title. PZ8.3.Q2Th 784.4 [E]   74-4283   ISBN-0-397-31585-6

A NOTE

In 1871 Chicago was a city of wooden buildings housing more than three hundred thousand people. During the first week of October of that year, fires kept flaring up all over the tinder-dry city, and the firemen were exhausted from fighting the flames. Then on a warm evening, October 8, at 8:45, a fire broke out at the O'Leary barn on the West Side of the city. This fire, spread by thirty-mile-an-hour winds, started America's greatest fire disaster—the Great Chicago Fire, in which most of the city was destroyed.

The Great Fire of 1871 raged for two days. The firemen's struggle to control the blaze was made even more difficult when the city's waterworks burned down. But on October 10 it rained, and the fire was put out. Two hundred and fifty people had lost their lives and twenty thousand homes had been destroyed, leaving ninety thousand people homeless. Aid was sent to the survivors from all over the world, so no one went without food or shelter during the ensuing winter. Within just four years, the city was rebuilt with stone and steel.

Balladeers went to work immediately after the fire, turning out topical lyrics that reflected the intense public interest in the catastrophe. The one that survives today is the lighthearted "There'll Be a Hot Time in the Old Town Tonight." The song refuses to take the fire seriously. It blames a cow for starting the fire by kicking over a lantern that Mrs. O'Leary, who was in bed with a sore foot, had placed in the barn earlier. The tune is derived from a folk melody that has been sung in America since the early 1800s, in many versions. It is sung enthusiastically today by college students, Boy Scouts, and children of all ages.

This popular folk song is the basis of the fifth picture-song book of Americana by Robert Quackenbush. He has based his illustrations on authentic prints and photographs of the period and has written additional verses to the song. He wishes to thank the Chicago Historical Society, the National Headquarters of the Boy Scouts of America, the New York City Firemen's Library and Museum, and the Manhattan and Queens Public Libraries for their help in making this book possible.

WATERWORKS

One dark night—when we were all in bed,

Mrs. O'Leary lit a lantern in the shed;

The cow kicked it over,

Then winked its eye, and said,

There'll be a hot time in the old town tonight.

Fire! Fire! Fire!—The shed is burning down!

Fire! Fire! Fire!—It's burning to the ground!

And when wind fanned the flames,

The word soon got around,

There'll be a hot time in the old town tonight.

Fetch the pails—and bring them to the shed,

Wake the kids—and get them out of bed;

And when we called Our Boys,

In unison they said,

There'll be a hot time in the old town tonight.

They were grim and their horses did perspire,

Jump her, boys! Get your steamers to the fire!

And when the flames rose high,

Their voices cried in ire,

There'll be a hot time in the old town tonight.

Red snow fell—the fire spread far and wide,

Our Brave Boys—the raging flames defied;

And when their hose went dry,

They looked about and sighed,

There'll be a hot time in the old town tonight.

Fire devils flared — like lightning in the air,

Homes caught fire — and left just ashes there;

And when the flames marched by,

We called out in the glare,

There'll be a hot time in the old town tonight.

Ruins! Ruins! Ruins! from the West to the North Side,

O'er the river — and to the prairie wide;

And when all fled to shore,

We shouted 'cross the tide,

There'll be a hot time in the old town tonight.

Raise our city! came the voices from the shore,
Build with steel, make it safer than before;
So when you lay the stones,
You'll hear these words no more,
There'll be a hot time in the old town tonight.

Rain! Rain! Rain! was what ended the torment,

Homes were gone, so we had to live in tents;

And when aid did come,

It was sent with this intent,

There'll be a hot time in the old town tonight.

SHED
JEFFERSON ST.
CHICAGO RIVER
DE KOVEN ST.
CHICAGO RIVER
FULLERTON AVE.
LAKE MICHIGAN
MILES
1   2
W
S   N
E

Fire and flame and a town of wood and frame,

Gone to glory — but left undying fame;

It was due to a lamp,

And a cow who made this claim,

There'll be a hot time in the old town tonight.

Heed this tale — that brought a cow to blame,

Don't strike fire, for it surely is no game;

But think kindly of the cow,

When you sing this next refrain,

There'll be a hot time in the old town tonight.

Shame, oh, shame, said the cow with this lament:

I'm to blame and I heartily repent!

And when I set the blaze,

I paid the consequence,

There'll be a cold time in the old town tonight.

One dark night — when we were all in bed,

Mrs. — O' Lear-y lit a lan-tern in the shed; The cow —

IN THE OLD TOWN TONIGHT

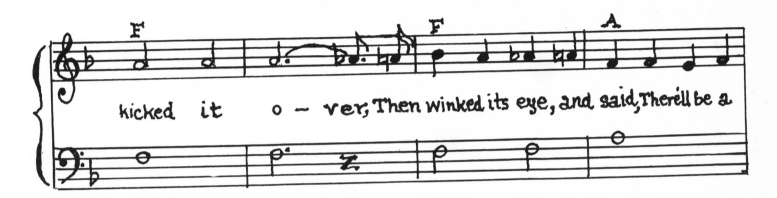

kicked it o — ver; Then winked its eye, and said, There'll be a

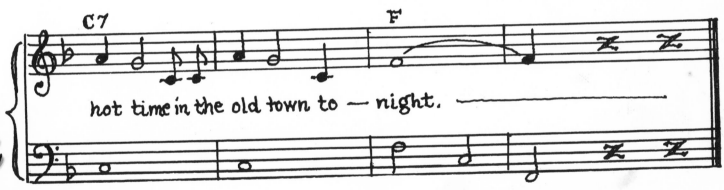

hot time in the old town to — night.

Arranged by Marguerite O. Daly

HERE IS YOUR OWN FIRE SURVIVAL PLAN

The people who lost their lives in the Great Chicago Fire were those who did not listen to the warnings of neighbors to leave their homes, or who went back for their belongings, or who had not planned an escape route to use in case of fire. The thousands of survivors used rules for safety. Study this Fire Survival Plan. Visit your local firemen to learn more about fires and fire prevention. Discuss with your parents and teachers ways you can help prevent fires.

HAVE A FAMILY FIRE PLAN

- DRAW A FLOOR PLAN.
- PLAN ESCAPES FROM ROOMS.
- PLAN TWO EXITS.
- MAKE SURE WINDOWS OR SCREENS IN ALTERNATE EXITS CAN OPEN EASILY.
- PLAN A MEETING PLACE OUTSIDE THE HOME IN A WELL-LIGHTED AREA.
- KEEP FLASHLIGHTS HANDY.
- ASSIGN RESPONSIBILITIES.
- HAVE A FAMILY FIRE DRILL ONCE A MONTH.

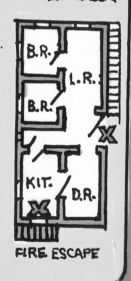

FIRE ESCAPE

IN CASE OF FIRE

ALERT OTHERS

•

DIAL "O"PERATOR AND GIVE EXACT LOCATION

•

PULL ALARM HANDLE THEN WAIT TO DIRECT FIREFIGHTERS

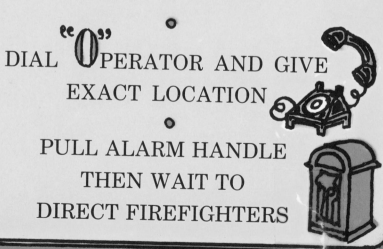

HOW TO ESCAPE FROM A BURNING BUILDING

LOCATE EXIT — Learn the nearest path of escape from home, school, other buildings. Report locked or obstructed exits to Fire Department.

GET OUT — It is always dangerous to remain in a burning building. Fires spread rapidly and cut off escape and are likely to generate poisonous gases.

KEEP CALM — If there is a panic-rush for the main exit, keep out of the crowd and attempt to find some other means of escape. Use stairs, not elevator which may stop and trap you.

KEEP LOW-HOLD BREATH — If forced to remain in a smoke-filled building, remember that the air is usually better near the floor. If you must make a dash through smoke or flame, hold your breath.

SAFE REFUGE-CALL FOR HELP — A temporary refuge may be secured behind any closed door. Try to pick a room with a window to the outside. Open the window at top and bottom. You can breathe and call for help at lower opening; smoke and heat will escape at the top.

DON'T JUMP — Do not jump from upper-story windows except as a last resort. Wait for firemen to bring ladders.

TEST CLOSED DOOR — Feel door with palm of hand; if door is hot, don't open it. If your palm detects no heat, door may be opened carefully. Keep your body behind door, with one hand held at opening. If air is hot or you feel pressure, slam door shut.

CLOSE DOOR ON FIRE — If you leave by the door, make sure that you close it behind you. This will limit amount of oxygen available to the fire and keep heated gases and fire from following you.

CAUGHT IN SMOKE — If caught in smoke, take short breaths, breathe through the nose. Crouch or crawl along floor to escape.

DON'T RE-ENTER — Don't take chances by re-entering a burning building to save your things. Leave the job of fire fighting to firemen.